THE NEW YET OLD MASS

THE NEW YET OLD MASS

JOSEPH M. CHAMPLIN

Ave Maria Press • Notre Dame, Indiana 46556

Acknowledgments:

English translation of excerpts from the Sacramentary. Copyright © 1973 by International Committee on English in the Liturgy, Inc. All rights reserved.

Excerpts from *Vatican Council II*—The Conciliar and Post Conciliar Documents, General Editor: Austin Flannery, O.P. Copyright © 1975 by Austin Flannery, O.P. and Harry Costello.

Nihil Obstat:
>Rev. John L. Roark
>Censor Deputatus

Imprimatur:
>Most Rev. Frank J. Harrison, D.D.
>Bishop of Syracuse

Library of Congress Catalog Card Number: 77-72286

International Standard Book Number: 0-87793-132-1

© 1977 by Ave Maria Press, Notre Dame, Indiana 46556 All rights reserved.

Photography:
>Alpha Corporation, 60; Joseph R. Fuzey, 14; Anthony Rowland, 36, 106.

Printed in the United States of America

Contents

Preface		7
Foreword		9
Introduction		11

PART 1: Introductory Rites

1.	A Praying Community in God's Presence	17
2.	A Time for Healing	20
3.	A Congregation Which Cares	23
4.	Silence and Mystery	26
5.	Words, Words, Words	29
6.	Prayer to the Father	32

PART 2: Liturgy of the Word

7.	God Present and Speaking	39
8.	A Daily Dialogue With God	42
9.	The Homily: A Living Explanation of the Word	45
10.	Comfortable and Confident Singers	48
11.	Preaching to Children	51
12.	Praying for Others	54
13.	Announcements and the Parish Bulletin	57

PART 3: Liturgy of the Eucharist

14.	Offering Symbolic Gifts	63
15.	The Offertory Procession	66
16.	Simple, But Symbolic Gestures	69
17.	An Ancient But Current Prayer	72
18.	Elements of the Eucharistic Prayer	75
19.	Our Holy Father and the Mass	78
20.	Communion of Saints	81
21.	The Coming of the Spirit	84
22.	The Lord's Prayer	87
23.	The Sign of Peace	90
24.	The Breaking of Bread	93
25.	The Risen Lamb of God	96
26.	Communion in the Hand and From the Cup	99
27.	Alone or Together	102

PART 4: Concluding Rites

28.	Go in Peace to Love and Serve the Lord	109

Preface

Four hundred years may seem like a long period of time for us, but in the history of the Roman Catholic Church such a span of centuries represents but a phase in its life. The altar book used for Mass in Catholic churches up until 1970 was just that old. Issued in 1570 by St. Pius V, the Roman Missal, published originally in Latin and with priests generally celebrating according to its rubrics in that language, could be found on altars everywhere in the world.

On April 3, 1969, Pope Paul VI released for the universal Church a new *Missale Romanum* or Roman Missal. This edition, completely revised according to the decree of the Second Vatican Ecumenical Council, is now obligatory wherever priests offer the Roman rite of our eucharistic liturgy.

American Catholics have already experienced the new, yet old, Mass for about a half dozen years. Nevertheless, the Eucharist remains a mystery and our understanding or, better, awareness of that sacred reality can always be deepened. I hope this little book may contribute to the deepening process.

Originally columns for the NC News Service Know Your Faith series, this material has been edited and joined in segments corresponding to the four sections of the restored liturgy: Introductory Rites, Liturgy of the Word, Liturgy of the Eucharist, Concluding Rites. An initial portion on the importance and dignity of the Eucharistic Celebration is an excerpt from the General Instruction of the Roman Missal.

These brief explanations examine each part of the Mass, offer some historical, theological and legal explanations, then suggest occasional practical ramifications for the typical congregation.

The text should, we trust, prove helpful for all those interested in growing to understand and love the Mass more perfectly: adult study groups, liturgical committees, parish councils, high school and college students, as well as priests and pastors.

I would like to thank my editor at Ave Maria Press as well as Miss Patricia Reilly of Fulton, New York, and Mrs. Jean Germano of Rome, Italy, who typed the original columns.

> Rev. Joseph M. Champlin
> Pastor-in-Residence, 1976-1977
> North American College
> Rome, Italy

Foreword

Importance and Dignity of the Eucharistic Celebration*

The celebration of Mass is the action of Christ and the people of God hierarchically assembled. For both the universal and the local Church, and for each person, it is the center of the whole Christian life. The Mass reaches the high point of the action by which God in Christ sanctifies the world and the high point of men's worship of the Father, as they adore him through Christ, his Son. During the course of the year the mysteries of redemption are recalled at Mass so that they are in some way made present. All other actions and works of the Christian life are related to the Eucharistic Celebration, leading up to it and flowing from it.

It is of the greatest importance that the celebration of the Mass, the Lord's Supper, be so arranged that the ministers and the faithful may take their own proper part in it and thus gain its fruits more fully. For this Christ the Lord instituted the eucharistic sacrifice of his body and blood and entrusted it to his bride, the Church, as a memorial of his passion and resurrection.

The purpose will be accomplished if the celebration takes into account the nature and circumstances of each assembly and is planned to bring about conscious, active, and full participation of the people, motivated by faith,

---
* From *The Roman Missal*, General Instruction, copyright © 1973, International Committee on English in the Liturgy Inc. Chapter 1.

hope, and charity. Such participation of mind and body is desired by the Church, is demanded by the nature of the celebration, and is the right and duty of Christians by reason of their baptism.

The presence and active participation of the people show plainly the ecclesial nature of the celebration. Although at times this participation may be lacking, the Eucharistic Celebration, in which the priest always acts for the salvation of the people, retains its efficacy and dignity as the action of Christ and the Church.

The celebration of the Eucharist, and the entire liturgy, is carried out by the use of outward signs. By these signs faith is nourished, strengthened, and expressed. It is thus very important to select and arrange the forms and elements proposed by the Church, which, taking into account individual and local circumstances, will best foster active and full participation and promote the spiritual welfare of the faithful.

This instruction is intended to give general guidelines for celebrating the Eucharist and also norms for each form of celebration. In accord with the Constitution on the Liturgy, each conference of bishops may establish additional norms for its territory to suit the traditions and character of the people, regions, and various communities.

Introduction

The parents of our First Communicants at Holy Family parish, Fulton, New York, gather in small groups at different homes for the second of their instruction classes. During the course of that session they view a filmstrip called *Understanding the Liturgy* which sketches the historical development of the Mass.

The reaction of these adults to this audiovisual always seems to be the same. "We never understood before that the changes in the liturgy being introduced now are not really something new, but more a going back to the old ways of the Church in the early Christian days."

They refer by such a comment to recent reforms like altars facing the people and congregational participation.

Those two developments and other similar liturgical revisions thus follow the principles for updating Catholic worship approved by the Second Vatican Council and published in the *Constitution on the Sacred Liturgy*. Article 23 states:

> That sound tradition may be retained, and yet the way be open for legitimate progress, a careful investigation is always to be made into each part of the liturgy which is to be revised. This investigation should be theological, historical, and pastoral. Also, the general laws govern-

ing the structure and meaning of the liturgy must be studied in conjunction with the experience derived from recent liturgical reforms and from the indults conceded to various places. Finally, there must be no innovations unless the good of the Church genuinely and certainly requires them, and care must be taken that any new forms adopted should in some way grow organically from forms already existing.

This book, in part, will consider that historical aspect of Roman Catholic liturgy. By examining "worship yesterday," we can, as our First Communion parents did, better understand "worship today."

The goal of liturgical reform, however, is not simply to recreate something from the past. Instead, "the aim to be considered before all else," in the words of Vatican II, is "full and active participation by all the people."

To achieve such involvement the Council Fathers recognized and directed that certain elements of the liturgy subject to change should be modified if they no longer help, but instead hinder, a congregation's full sharing in the Sacred Mysteries.

This book, by describing actual examples of successful "worship today" around the United States, will attempt to illustrate how concerned parishes or worshiping communities are adapting the liturgy in that fashion to meet current circumstances.

Finally, in these chapters we will occasionally peek at "worship tomorrow."

The Church is a pilgrim Church always on the move. As members of such a changing body, we must be careful about clinging to practices which are not essential, but accidental. Not all change is progress, but all progress does involve change.

Catholic worship will remain fairly stable for a few

Introduction

years at least. The reform of major liturgical books has been completed. But, again as noted in the Liturgy Constitution, articles 37-40, the Church allows bishops in each country to make further substantial or radical adaptations of rituals, if particular needs of the people demand them.

Time will tell just how much of this adapting we can expect in the United States. For example, will there be additional Eucharistic Prayers? Will the official translations of liturgy texts be improved, made less sexist? Will Communion in the hand become an accepted practice in our country? Will permanent deacons anoint the sick? Will general absolution be more common?

The New, Yet Old, Mass shall consider some of these possibilities for the future as well as explore how our present liturgy has its roots in the past.

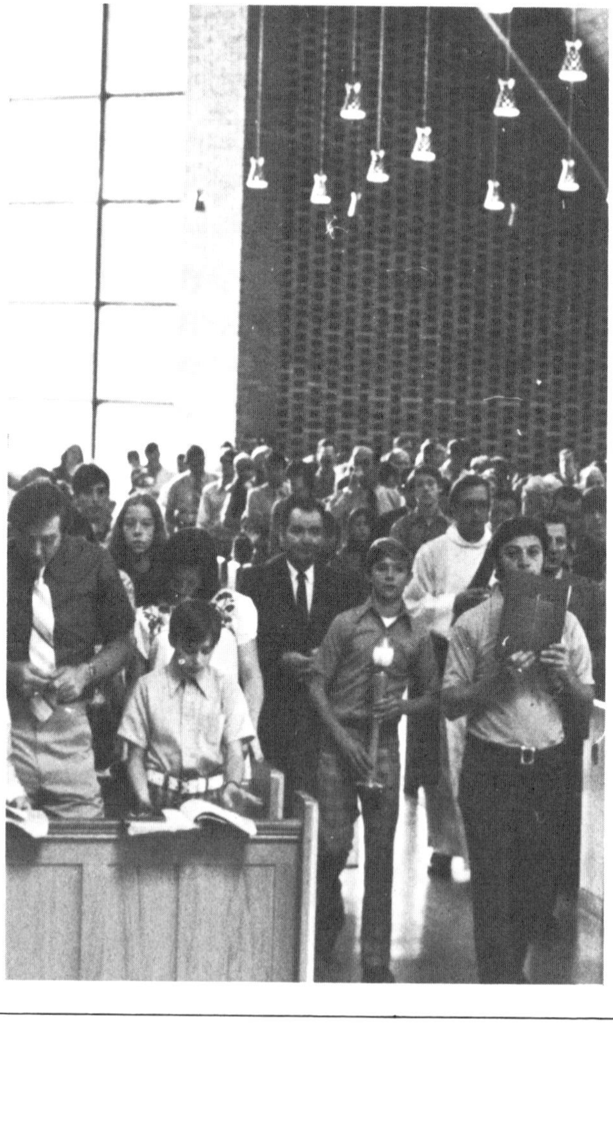

PART I:
Introductory Rites

General Structure of the Mass

The Lord's Supper or Mass gathers together the people of God, with a priest presiding in the person of Christ, to celebrate the memorial of the Lord or eucharistic sacrifice. For this reason the promise of Christ is particularly true of such a local congregation of the Church: "Where two or three are gathered in my name, there am I in their midst" (Matthew 18:20). In the celebration of Mass, which perpetuates the sacrifice of the cross, Christ is really present in the assembly itself, which is gathered in his name, in the person of the minister, in his word, and indeed substantially and unceasingly under the eucharistic species.

Although the Mass is made up of the liturgy of the word and the liturgy of the Eucharist, the two parts are so closely connected as to form one act of worship. The table of God's word and of Christ's body is prepared and from it the faithful are instructed and nourished. In addition, the Mass has introductory and concluding rites.

The parts preceding the liturgy of the word, namely, the entrance song, greeting, penitential rite, Kyrie, Gloria, and opening prayer or collect, have the character of beginning, introduction, and preparation.

The purpose of these rites is to make the assembled people a unified community and to prepare them properly to listen to God's word and celebrate the Eucharist.

—*The Roman Missal,* General Instruction

1. A Praying Community in God's Presence

We come to church for Mass in various moods: sometimes tired and sleepy, usually preoccupied with personal concerns, and often quite isolated from or unaware of those others who have gathered for the same purpose.

The Introductory Rites of our revised eucharistic liturgy seek to deal with these attitudes. Those ceremonies attempt to stir us up, to lead us gently from our daily preoccupations into an atmosphere of prayer and to form out of separated individuals a worshiping community.

For years I have spent the 15 minutes prior to Mass either standing out in front of church or walking from pew to pew greeting parishioners. This is a fatiguing and occasionally awkward task, but the labor bears rich fruit in many ways. It lifts people out of their isolation and can give them a warm sense of belonging.

But the priest or parish helper who does this type of welcoming should exercise a certain reserve or care in that function.

From the first Christian days those pre-Mass moments have been opportunities for the faithful to become recollected, to leave aside their noisy, busy, troubled worlds and to grow in awareness of God's special presence at the celebration. An early church law in Egypt, for example, directed the psalms to be recited while the faithful arrived;

in our day, private or public recitation of the rosary, the reading of devotional prayers, or just quiet reflection serves a parallel purpose.

The greeter, then, must have a delicate touch, working to build a community, but not intruding much on those precious minutes of intimate, silent, highly personal, preparatory prayer.

However, the introductory rites do have as their purpose "to make the assembled people a unified community." The Eucharist is a communal celebration and group worship.

The entrance song helps achieve that goal. Its function, again to quote the Roman Missal's General Introduction, is "to open the celebration, deepen the unity of the people, introduce them to the mystery of the season or feast, and accompany the procession" (Articles 24-25).

Catholic and Protestant music directors would do well to get together on this matter. We Catholics generally sing too few verses for the hymn to achieve its community and theme-developing effect; Protestant worship contrariwise normally insists on every verse, even to the point of the congregation's exhaustion.

A celebrant's "good morning, everyone" after his reverent kiss of the altar and the congregation's comfortable response to that greeting likewise aids in generating a community feeling. At Holy Family we also now and then invite the congregation to introduce themselves to their neighbors in the pews.

The group of people gathered for worship, nevertheless, is more than a mere secular assembly or a purely human group.

The sign of the cross, that most renowned symbol of our faith and of the Trinity, begins the formal liturgy and is immediately followed by a scriptural greeting.

Introductory Rites

The latter either speaks to the people as St. Paul did to the Christians in Corinth or follows a common formula taken from Old Testament times (Ruth 2:4). That phrase, "The Lord be with you," aptly declares God is truly present in this family of believers assembled in his name (Mt 18:20; 28:20).

"This greeting and the people's response manifest the mystery of the Church that is gathered together" (General Introduction, article 28).

Such a transition from the noisy world through quiet prayer to a communal spirit and the sense of our Lord's presence requires some time. It also presupposes a prayerful approach and a belief in the sacred or transcendent.

A priest with those qualities who processes down the full center aisle, reverences the altar with care, welcomes his people warmly and greets them with a message of faith will have well prepared the congregation for God's Word and Body which follow.

2. A Time for Healing

Coming together as God's family,
with confidence let us ask the Father's forgiveness,
for he is full of gentleness and compassion.

That invitation to repent, one of three official versions contained in our Roman Missal, leads into the Penitential Rite of Mass. It acknowledges that all of us are sinners—bruised and wounded persons in need of healing. During this brief ritual we confess our sinfulness in a general way as a group or community and seek the Lord's pardon.

Here are a few observations about the revised penitential service:

* This is not intended to replace or to be the occasion for the sacrament of Penance. Instead, the Church wishes it to serve as a time to admit we are sinners even while we hope we are in God's good graces.

There are strong theological, liturgical, legal and pastoral reasons why the Church discourages the sacrament of reconciliation or Penance within Mass. That type of healing best belongs in a different situation. Nevertheless, the Penitential Rite itself has the power both to forgive our lesser faults and dispose us for God's saving action later in the eucharistic liturgy.

* The shorter, simpler "Confiteor" or "I confess to almighty God" of our present missal represents a return to one of the oldest formulas in the Church's tradition.

Introductory Rites 21

It brings out more clearly two notions about our own sinfulness.

First of all, sin not only ruptures our relationship with God, it also breaks or weakens our bond with others. Sin's vertical dimension, "I confess to almighty God," has in the past been quite evident to us; sin's horizontal aspect, "and to you, my brothers and sisters," was not always so keenly stressed or apparent to Catholic Christians. The restored formula links both together in a more correct balance.

Secondly, the new Confiteor reminds us that we can sin by omission as well as commission. "In what I have done, and in what I have failed to do" succinctly recalls, particularly through the last phrase, Jesus' warning that he was hungry, thirsty, or in trouble and we did not respond. "As often as you neglected to do it to one of these least ones, you neglected to do it for me."

* I frequently notice priests and, consequently, other participants, sign themselves with the cross at the words,

May almighty God have mercy on us,
forgive us our sins,
and bring us to everlasting life.

There is nothing drastically wrong about that gesture at this point, but it simply is not called for by the missal's directions. Moreover, it does mar the work of simplification accomplished by the Vatican II liturgical decree. Article 34, for example, states: "The rites should be distinguished by a noble simplicity. They should be short, clear, and free from useless repetitions."

When I first learned how to offer Mass over 20 years ago, there were some 50 signs of the cross within the celebration. Pope Paul VI's Roman Missal calls for this gesture only at the beginning of Mass, over the gifts and at the liturgy's conclusion. Better to make this sacred sign a few times well and carefully, than many times poorly and in a hurry.

* The third form of the Penitential Rite, e.g.,

Lord Jesus, you healed the sick:
Lord, have mercy.

Lord Jesus, you forgave sinners:
Christ, have mercy.

Lord Jesus, you give us yourself to heal us and bring us strength:
Lord, have mercy.

is a litany of praise for the Lord which also implores his mercy.

The eight models given indicate the pattern which should be followed when celebrants and liturgy committees compose original versions.

The invocations, addressed to Christ, ought to be brief, direct and adapted to the season, feast or day's Gospel.

While sometimes referring to the reconciling, healing mission of Jesus, they should not, however, be turned into a kind of confession of sins or examination of conscience.

Since the revised Mass's introduction, this latter development has become common in our country. "For the times we have . . . . Lord, have mercy." That approach is very appropriate in a penance service, but not for the Penitential Rite of Mass.

3. A Congregation Which Cares

The letter which follows illustrates what I consider to be one of the major challenges facing the Church today: how do we transform usually huge, often impersonal parish congregations into communities of truly interested, warm and caring Christian believers?

"For the past two years I have been attending a small nondenominational church in addition to going to Mass. I have discovered what it is like to talk about Christ, to share him with other human beings. I have grown much closer to God through this non-Catholic Christian fellowship.

"I find this sense of community in some Catholic circles. I have seen it at retreats and in Catholic college centers. Yet it is not present in Sunday Mass—which is the first place it should be. As a community of believers, we are to strengthen each other in our common belief. Yet I feel and see no common bond with the people I sit next to on Sunday. We do not encourage each other verbally.

"I see this community developing in charismatic Catholic groups. Yet I hesitate to get involved in this. God's Spirit is much broader—he does much more than speak in tongues. Besides I think I need more emphasis on the greatest gift God has given me—Love, '1 Corinthians 13 love,' before I want to go on to the others.

"I believe in the beginnings of the Catholic Church—in how she has handed down her doctrines. It is the local parish—the majority of Catholic people—I no longer have as much faith in. I see these people on Friday or Saturday night using our Lord's name every other sentence. And they certainly aren't speaking in favor of him! I ask God to show me how I am to have faith and trust in these fellow Catholics I sit next to. *Are these really God's chosen people?* Is the Catholic Church teaching them what God can do for them? Are we simply talking about love and not being love?

"In the nondenominational church I do not believe in their doctrine—yet I do believe in the people there. They are living every day for Christ—he isn't with them only on Sundays.

"When God shows me which of these last two areas—doctrine or honesty and fellowship—a church family is supposed to be strongest in, my decision will be made. Till then I continue to search and pray for the strength God gives."

The Church proposes as an ideal what my torn and distressed correspondent seeks to find in practice at Catholic parishes. Article 62 of the Roman Missal's introduction, for example, states:

"In the celebration of Mass the faithful form a holy people, a chosen race, a royal priesthood: they give thanks to the Father and offer the victim not only through the hands of the priest but also with him, and they learn to offer themselves. They should make this clear by their deep sense of religion and their charity to everyone who shares in the celebration."

An attitudinal change and increased awareness on the part of individual Catholics ultimately seem the answer.

Introductory Rites

"Charity to everyone who shares in the celebration" is merely a different, more technical way of describing people who truly care about others in the parish, who speak to them before and after Mass, who pray from the heart during the liturgy and who later eagerly volunteer to serve those in any kind of need. For such persons, their Sunday worship carries over into everyday living.

Division of mammoth parishes into more manageable units, however, also appears highly desirable, even critically necessary. It is very questionable whether the kind of personally concerned Christians sought for by this letter writer would be evident and dominant in our extremely large churches. Needless to say, the God who is preached, worshiped and experienced in such settings may likewise strike many as cold, indifferent and impersonal.

4. Silence and Mystery

When I first offered Mass over 20 years ago I stood at a massive marble altar with my back to the congregation, prayed in the Latin language, and occasionally turned toward the people. They generally remained silent.

A few whispered the proper Latin responses, some privately read the Mass texts from small weekly or large daily missals, others fingered rosary beads, still others just knelt or sat and gazed at the Sacred Mystery being re-enacted before them in the sanctuary.

I am not anxious to return to those days of quiet liturgies and mostly silent worshipers. The Church's desire for active participation in word, song and deed has my enthusiastic support.

However, I am also not about to criticize severely or reject totally what was done in those years from 1940 to 1950. People then did pray at Mass, and an atmosphere of reverence, awe and mystery tended to prevail.

In reforming Catholic worship, the Vatican II Fathers stated: "To promote active participation, the people should be encouraged to take part by means of acclamations, responses, psalms, hymns, as well as by actions, gestures and bodily attitudes. And at the proper time a reverent silence should be observed" (Article 30).

Introductory Rites

Note the last sentence: "And at the proper time a reverent silence should be observed."

Unfortunately, as so often occurs in human history, the pendulum swings from one extreme to the other. During the last decade liturgies at least in the United States seemed to have moved from a "silent Mass" stage to the "noisy Mass" era.

Many planners and executers of eucharistic worship appear to have overreacted and become anxious to fill each second of every Mass with something spoken, sung or done. When an interval of silence inadvertently develops, they grow uneasy and rush to remedy the situation.

This certainly is not the mind of the Church as expressed in the Roman Missal produced according to the directives of the Second Vatican Council.

Its General Instruction very clearly notes: "Silence should be observed at designated times as part of the celebration."

Article 23 then pinpoints some of the suitable occasions. "Its character will depend on the time it occurs in the particular celebration. At the penitential rite and again after the invitation to pray, each one should become recollected; at the conclusion of a reading or the homily, each one meditates briefly on what he has heard; after communion, he praises God in his heart and prays."

I find frequently that lectors completely disregard this point after the first scriptural reading. As soon as the reader declares, "This is the word of the Lord," he or she immediately takes up the responsorial psalm. At Holy Family we encourage the lector to recite at this point the Our Father quietly and then move on. It works effectively to slow down the celebration and to provide the desired period of silent reflection.

The Mass rubrics rather clearly demonstrate how a

silent pause fits into the opening prayer or collect.

"Next the priest invites the people to pray, and together they spend some moments in silence so they may realize that they are in God's presence and may make their petitions. The priest then says the prayer which is called the opening prayer or collect" (Article 32).

Some celebrants I have observed likewise either omit the silent pause or so abbreviate the silence that it has little meaning. The period for silent prayer and reflection should not be too extensive, but long enough for the congregation to understand what the hesitation is for and to use the pause accordingly.

One point is certain: proper periods of silence in Mass are essential for recapturing that sense of mystery experienced in the 40's and 50's.

5. Words, Words, Words

At an ecumenical graduation service a few years back, one of the clergymen introduced his benediction in the usual manner: "Let us pray."

We all stood, bowed our heads and prepared to listen in a reverent spirit for this concluding prayer of the ceremony. My colleague's invocation, however, became more of a sermon. It went on and on and on.

I strongly disapprove of clergy in the sanctuary looking at their watches within the course of a liturgy and I attempt to resist that impulse myself when serving as a celebrant. But as his benediction continued, my legs grew weary and my restless mind wandered, I finally yielded to the temptation. A swift and concealed glance at my watch (head still bowed), indicated the prayer was now into its seventh minute.

This event reminded me of the late Cardinal Cushing's invocation at the inaugural of President John F. Kennedy. That prayer likewise seemed interminable and I believe only a fire in the lectern brought the oration to a halt.

In our multimedia age, with television such a dominant means of communication and entertainment, visual images generally tell the story; words usually but accompany the pictures and tend to hold secondary importance.

During the televised "Statio Orbis" Mass concluding the 1976 Eucharistic Congress, for example, the cameras began to look for other scenes of interest—the crowd, flashbacks, the President—while Cardinal Knox delivered his homily. Straight talk on TV lacks the power to sustain interest. Words, words, words and the viewer flips to another program; the same could be true of those who worship—their minds may switch to another channel when the liturgy becomes too wordy.

This is one of the dangers in spontaneous, extemporaneous public prayer on the part of celebrants or leaders of worship. It takes careful preparation to speak succinctly, to use a minimum of words, to say much with a few, well-chosen phrases. Otherwise, we normally are very verbose.

I am not referring here to nonliturgical prayer gatherings which have grown rapidly in recent years. More extensive and subjective praying out loud in those specialized circumstances may well have power and impact. Instead, these observations apply to official worship, e.g., the rituals for Mass and the sacraments, or to generalized public services, such as the graduation event mentioned earlier.

The Roman Missal, especially in its prayers or orations, usually follows that pattern of paucity in word use. The "collects" are brief, their phrases few and universal in scope.

In theory, the congregation has been invited to pray silently and very personally for a short period of time. Then, the celebrant, speaking in their name, collects or sums up the many individual, private intentions and presents them to the Father through Jesus our mediator in the Holy Spirit. A short, concise, objective prayer can do that; a lengthy, subjective oration tends to take the congregation in a different direction.

The opening prayer for the 29th Sunday in Ordinary Time illustrates the Missal's brevity:

> Almighty and ever-living God,
> our source of power and inspiration,
> give us strength and joy
> in serving you as followers of Christ,
> who lives and reigns with you and the Holy Spirit,
> one God, forever and ever.

The alternative opening prayer for that Sunday is more expansive, but still reflects the same principles of succinctness:

> Lord our God, Father of all,
> you guard us under the shadow of your wings
> and search into the depths of our hearts.
> Remove the blindness that cannot know you
> and relieve the fear that would hide us from your sight.
> We ask this through Christ our Lord.

6. Prayer to the Father

I joined five couples the other night at a home in our parish for a combination "after the meeting let's relax" and "before a big event we wish you well" kind of session.

Two of the couples had been commissioned a few weeks earlier as special ministers of Holy Communion to the sick. That evening they joined the other 10 ministers in the church hall to evaluate those initial Sunday visits to the ill, to share their reactions, to make practical plans for the future and to view filmstrips on the Eucharist and Penance. Now at 10:30, they were sitting on the floor of this house unwinding in the midst of several persons especially close to them.

One of the couples had returned earlier in the week from a "deeper" Marriage Encounter. Selected to become a member of teams who present the talks on regular M.E. weekends, this husband and wife traveled to New York for that special three-day training experience. They were still floating on a cloud or, perhaps more accurately, were still tasting the profound spiritual peace of those 44 hours.

Another couple, our host and hostess, would leave the next afternoon for Syracuse to "give" a M.E. weekend. Their talks were written and had been carefully critiqued by veteran couples in the movement. However, the anticipation of sitting before 25 new couples, quite intimately revealing one's self to them, and hoping the experience will touch these husbands and wives leaves any presenting couple anxious. We were on hand to support Pat and Donna with our presence and prayers.

The last couple, a veteran "presenting" husband and wife scheduled for a weekend several months later, understood and shared the feelings of those present.

Before leaving we all, in a frequently practiced Marriage Encounter tradition, formed a close circle and prayed. The prayer was informal, spontaneous, personal and addressed to the Father. Each one participated.

"Thank you, Father, for this evening and for humor."

"Father, bless Pat and Donna and the couples they will touch this weekend."

"Take care of our father, Father, as he leaves for Rome."

"Help the sick we visit."

"Thank you, Father, for giving us one another."

None of those couples two years earlier would have prayed like that. They were then and are now excellent Catholics and active parishioners. But such open, shared prayer to our Father in heaven was not a pattern in their lives.

Archbishop Jean Jadot, Pope Paul's representative in the United States, sees in the charismatic movement and in marriage encounter two great signs of renewal in the Church. My own experience with M.E. leads me to agree strongly with him in that observation. It was the marriage encounter weekend and follow-up programs which brought those five couples to such a desire for an openness in prayer to the Father.

The liturgical reforms rather neatly coincide with this emphasis on our relationship to the Father.

Revisions in the Prefaces and Eucharistic Prayers, for example, restore the original notion that the Mass is worship of the Father through Christ our mediator in the Holy Spirit. Notice, during Sunday Mass, how often the word "Father" occurs.

The opening prayer also illustrates that point. As a conclusion to the Introductory Rites, it "expresses the theme of the celebration; by the words of the priest a petition is addressed to God the Father through the mediation of Christ in the Holy Spirit" (General Instruction, article 32).

The celebrant with hands outstretched (sending our petitions heavenward and hoping to receive God's gifts in response), speaks as a general rule directly to the Father in the collect's beginning.

"Almighty and ever-living God."

"God of power and mercy."

"Father of all that is good."

We, standing out of respect for the risen Lord, lend our agreement to this prayer and petition to the Father with a loud "Amen" at the end.

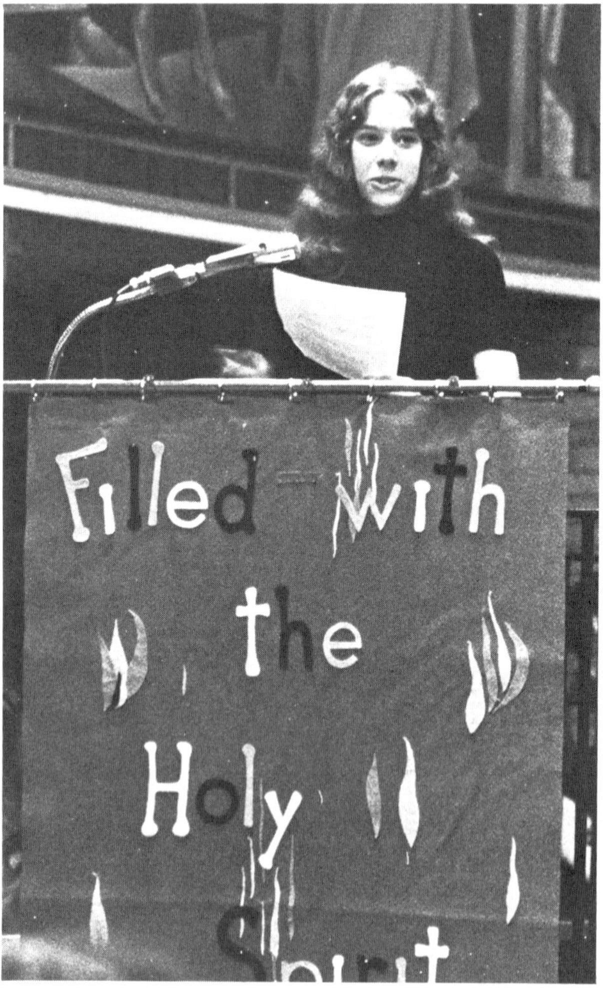
Filled with
the
Holy

PART II:
Liturgy of the Word

Liturgy of the Word

Readings from scripture and the chants between the readings form the main part of the liturgy of the word. The homily, profession of faith, and general intercessions or prayer of the faithful develop and complete it. In the readings, explained by the homily, God speaks to his people of redemption and salvation and nourishes their spirit; Christ is present among the faithful through his word. Through the chants the people make God's word their own and express their adherence to it through the profession of faith. Finally, moved by his word, they pray in the general intercessions for the needs of the Church and for the world's salvation.

—*The Roman Missal,* General Instruction

7. God Present and Speaking

One of the finer homilies my partner at Holy Family, Father David Baehr, has given since his arrival here a year ago touched on the question of God's presence in our midst.

He captured the congregation's interest very cleverly at the beginning by citing several instances in which we can be present to another person even though not physically before that individual.

A long-distance, low-rate, late-at-night telephone call between two persons who care about each other is an example. In a sense we become present to one another in that fashion through the sound of our voices.

A letter from me to you serves as another illustration. I become present before the eyes of your mind and imagination as you read the words I have written.

Neither of these ways measures up to the richness or intensity of actual physical presence, but there can be no doubt that I am really present to you through a telephone visit or a lengthy letter.

The following text—article 7 from Vatican II's *Constitution on the Sacred Liturgy*—about Christ's divine presence in our midst makes better sense when considered in the light of these parallels involving different human presences.

To accomplish so great a work Christ is always present in his Church, especially in her liturgical celebrations. He is present in the Sacrifice of the Mass not only in the person of his minister, "the same now offering, through the ministry of priests, who formerly offered himself on the cross," but especially in the eucharistic species. By his power he is present in the sacraments, so that when anybody baptizes it is really Christ himself who baptizes. He is present in his word since it is he himself who speaks when the holy scriptures are read in the Church. Lastly, he is present when the Church prays and sings, for he has promised "where two or three are gathered together in my name there am I in the midst of them."

These doctrinal statements have practical ramifications. Because we believe God speaks to us in a unique way through sacred scripture, becomes present to and in the congregation, every Eucharist contains a Liturgy of the Word prior to the breaking of bread.

In the biblical readings of that section, "explained by the homily, God speaks to his people of redemption and salvation and nourishes their spirit; Christ is present among the faithful through his word. Through the chants the people make God's word their own and express their adherence to it through the profession of faith" (*The Roman Missal*'s General Instruction, article 33).

Weak, doubting, flesh and blood creatures that we are, the Church surrounds the proclaiming of God's holy words of scripture with visible symbols and gestures which help remind us of Christ's powerful, although invisible, presence in the biblical texts.

* The scriptural passages should be read by the lector from large, handsome, ritual books (the Lectionary), not off a piece of typed paper or out of a pamphlet.

Liturgy of the Word

* "By standing to hear the reading and by their acclamations, the people recognize and acknowledge that Christ is present and speaking to them."

* We sign ourselves on forehead and lips as well as over the heart indicating our mind is open to receive Christ's word, that we are ready to confess it with our lips and, above all, we believe the message in our hearts.

* A procession with candles and incense speaks silently of the scriptural passages' dignity and importance.

* The people's acclamations before and after the Gospel are addressed directly to Christ, explicitly acknowledging his presence in the word.

"Glory to you, Lord."

"Praise to you, Lord Jesus Christ."

If we believe the Lord Jesus Christ is truly present in his word, then when that word speaks, as it often does, of mercy and compassion, we can know with certainty God forgives us.

8. A Daily Dialogue with God

The Mass before Vatican II contained readings from sacred scripture, but the selections varied little or not at all from day to day and from year to year.

That lack of variety prompted the Council Fathers to publish this directive in the *Constitution on the Sacred Liturgy:*

"The treasures of the Bible are to be opened up more lavishly so that a richer fare may be provided for the faithful at the table of God's Word. In this way a more representative part of the sacred scriptures will be read to the people in the course of a prescribed number of years" (Article 5).

The scholars who executed this recommendation did a masterful piece of work. Proof of that rests in the fact that many non-Roman Catholic Christian Churches have adopted in substance the revised lectionary of biblical texts for their own congregations.

The daily Mass-goer, over a three-year period, will thus hear excerpts from almost all Old and New Testament books. In addition, major texts and Gospel passages are repeated more frequently, usually on an annual basis.

The readings have been arranged according to somewhat involved principles. Ordinary Sundays throughout

Liturgy of the Word

the year are on a three-year basis; weekday celebrations during that season follow a two-year cycle; Advent, Lent and Easter scriptures appear, practically speaking, in the liturgy annually.

Such a richer inclusion of biblical texts within official worship has this as its purpose: "Hence in order to achieve the restoration, progress, and adaptation of the sacred liturgy it is essential to promote that sweet and living love for sacred scripture to which the venerable tradition of Eastern and Western rites gives testimony" (Article 24).

Those scriptural texts, assembled together in one book, provide not only a richer fare of reading for public worship, but also a readily available collection of inspired passages for personal prayer.

Cardinal Suenens, in his book, *A New Pentecost?* encourages believers to use the lectionary as a resource for daily meditation. He sees the Holy Spirit's guidance behind the gathering of those many experts and thus expects prayerful reflection on these texts will produce abundant spiritual fruit.

A helpful procedure in this regard is to keep a relatively inexpensive daily and Sunday missal near your reading chair or bed. Before retiring, peruse tomorrow's assigned passages and pick out a sentence or two which seem to evoke some kind of response within you.

The next day find a few moments and a place where you can be quiet and undisturbed; take out the missal or lectionary and stir up your awareness that this is God's word, that Jesus will now be speaking to you, that the Holy Spirit wishes to touch your heart through these phrases.

Then read the biblical excerpts over again, slowly and reflectively. Next, go back and read them once more, but this time pause at any passage which moves your inner self. Pause, taste, reflect, pray. If a certain section strikes you, simply turn it over and over in your mind.

Those lines selected in advance the evening before usually will hold the greatest attractiveness during this prayer and will linger on afterwards during the working day.

Many who have written on prayer and the inner life urge concerned Christians to jot down these favorite passages in a personal journal for future use.

Persons who practice that daily scriptural dialogue with God will discover how it enhances both their private prayer and the day's Eucharist. The daily Mass readings take on a deeper meaning when prepared the night before and prayed over beforehand.

9. The Homily: A Living Explanation of the Word

Many preachers today still have the habit of beginning a homily and concluding it with a sign of the cross.

In some ways that seems a praiseworthy practice. After all, this gesture is probably the most common Catholic symbol and contains within it our major beliefs—the oneness of God, the Trinity, the coming of Christ into the world, the Lord's death and resurrection, the dignity of Baptism.

However, there were sound reasons why the Vatican's Office for Divine Worship, in a commentary several years ago, discouraged starting and ending sermons with a sign of the cross. Such a procedure gives the impression a homily is distinctly separate from rather than an integral part of the total liturgy.

The Church, on the contrary, suggests the preacher's words should flow from the Gospel and lead into the Creed or Prayer of the Faithful.

Thus article 9 of the *Roman Missal*'s General Instruction reads: "In the biblical readings God's word is addressed to all men of every era and is understandable in itself, but a homily, as a living explanation of the word, increases its effectiveness and is an integral part of the service."

Article 41 speaks in similar terms: "The homily is

strongly recommended as an integral part of the liturgy and as a necessary source of nourishment of the Christian life."

Should the homily tackle current topics or restrict itself to an explanation and exegesis of the scriptural texts? Are sermons centering on a Mother's Day theme, or treating lay ministers of Communion or explaining the new rite of Penance out of order? Must the preacher concentrate on the Mass's biblical passages and simply try to develop a point or two from those excerpts?

The Roman Missal answers those questions with these words of article 41: "It should develop some point of the readings or of another text from the Ordinary of the Mass of the day. The homilist should keep in mind the mystery that is being celebrated and the needs of the particular community."

That response would appear to offer the preacher considerable freedom in fashioning his homily. There ought to be a connection with the scriptures of the liturgy, but matters of immediate concern to the worshiping community are certainly appropriate topics for the sermon.

In our liturgy planning sessions at Holy Family we have followed both patterns. Sometimes we simply go to the biblical texts and draw from them a point or two as the main theme for that weekend's Masses and homilies. On other occasions, we fit subjects which need consideration, e g., death and dying or the question of God's love and human suffering, into Sundays whose scriptural passages bear a certain relation to those particular issues.

Lay persons in the parish can serve as invaluable resource people for the homilist as he prepares his next weekend's sermons.

For instance, prior to Father's Day I asked Jack and Joan Pauldine if they would assist me in developing a suitable homily for the occasion. This couple in turn asked a

Liturgy of the Word

neighbor to join with them in gathering ideas for the topic.

After appointments in the rectory one evening, I stopped at their home around 9:15 and we spent the next hour and a half in an extremely beneficial discussion of what is or ought to be a "father."

They had done their homework. Jack took out a whole list of points jotted down since my phone call; his wife and the neighbor, Julie Patrick, likewise showed through their responses the lengthy reflection they gave the issue.

I furiously took notes of ideas and suggestions and stories. On Saturday morning an hour or two in prayer enabled me to sift through all those notions and pull them together in a homily.

The sermon's conclusion was really Jack's: "Be good to your father before it is too late. For sooner than you think, he will be gone. Then he will not see your tears as you stand by the tomb or hear your apologies at the side of his grave."

10. Comfortable and Confident Singers

The 8:00 a.m. weekday Mass at St. Columban's Cathedral in the industrial city of Youngstown, Ohio, draws a gathering of believers typical for that hour in the day. Ten to 20 persons assemble in or near the side Blessed Sacrament alcove of this handsome structure for the early morning liturgy.

Despite the sleepy hour and the absence of organ accompaniment, these worshipers do sing. The celebrant or, if he comes, a combination lector-leader-of-song-server announces the page number of the entrance melody. Then with large, recently purchased hymnals in hand, the community breaks out into an appropriate introductory song ("Ode to Joy" the day I concelebrated).

On occasion we attempt something similar for the 9:15 a.m. or 5:15 p.m. weekday celebrations at Holy Family, but instead of hymnals employ the monthly Mass booklets.

Leaders of worship who encourage this type of congregational response and those who participate in it are following both an ancient tradition and a modern Church directive.

Article 19 of the Roman Missal's General Instruction states: "The faithful who gather to await the Lord's com-

Liturgy of the Word

ing are urged by the Apostle Paul to sing psalms, hymns, and inspired songs (see Colossians 3:16). Song is the sign of the heart's joy (see Acts 2:46), and St. Augustine said: 'To sing belongs to lovers.' Even in antiquity it was proverbial to say, 'He prays twice who sings well.'

"Singing should be used widely at Mass, depending on the type of people and the capability of each congregation, but it is not always necessary to sing all the texts which were composed for singing."

The type and degree of singing thus will vary from celebration to celebration. Those weekday liturgies we described are not as solemn as Sunday Masses. So, too, our 5:15 p.m. and 8:30 a.m. weekend Eucharists include less congregational song than the major services at 9:45 and 11:15 on that day.

Comfortableness and confidence are the key to full music participation by a community. Those small clusters of people at Youngstown and Fulton were generally disposed to begin congregational song because of their familiarity and comfortableness with one another. As verse followed verse, the volume increased and hesitant singers joined the braver ones—both individuals and the group felt a growing confidence in their ability to handle this hymn.

Antiphonal singing (choir/cantor and the congregation) of the psalm which follows the first reading is an excellent method for building up that comfortableness and confidence.

The choir or cantor sings the brief refrain through once, then the congregation repeats this phrase. The choir and/or cantor next chants the psalm with the congregation responding after every verse or two by a repetition of the beginning antiphon or refrain.

I have experienced many instances in which the congregation started in very weak, timid fashion, but when the psalm was finished and they had sung the antiphon or refrain a half dozen times, the participation developed into a full, strong, confident response.

The Alleluia before our Gospel texts is also a highly effective vehicle for the facilitation of community singing. Its exchange between choir and congregation parallels the pattern for a responsorial psalm.

Alleluia, is, however, intended to be sung, not recited. Many congregations and their leaders seem to be unaware of article 39 which declares: "The alleluia or the verse before the Gospel may be omitted if not sung." The merely spoken recitation of one alleluia by priest and then by the congregation, a rather common practice in the United States, leaves something to be desired.

11. Preaching to Children

In any parish with several priests we normally find the younger clergy relate best to the children and teenagers. They are closer to them in age, share more of their interests and possess that joy, enthusiasm and interest which attract youth.

Jesuit Father Richard P. English is an exception to the rule or perhaps proof that one can be young in heart and spirit, even if older in years.

For the first two decades of his priesthood, Father English conducted retreats for individuals in their teens, initially at Gonzaga Retreat House in Monroe, New York, and then at St. Ignatius outside Buffalo.

His superiors, after those 20 years, gave him a sabbatical, an opportunity for several months of study and research. He put the time to good use, updating his theology and getting a clear picture of the best in post-Vatican II thought.

When that renewal period had been completed, Father English accepted an assignment as associate pastor at a parish in Florida. Almost immediately he began a weekly liturgy for children on Sunday. With careful and creative planning the Jesuit found he could, by means of these special Masses, communicate today's theology to the children and through them to the adults.

Many adaptations were necessary. In making these changes, Father English followed principles contained in the Roman *Directory for Masses with Children.*

For example, he normally employs only one scriptural reading, the Gospel. Article 42 supports that approach: "If three or even two readings on Sundays or weekdays can be understood by children only with difficulty, it is permissible to read two or only one of them, but the reading of the gospel should never be omitted."

Article 48 states: "The homily in which the word of God is unfolded should be given great prominence in all Masses with children. Sometimes the homily intended for children should become a dialogue with them, unless it is preferred that they should listen in silence."

Father English has taken those words to heart. His homilies, based on Ignatian principles for reflective meditation and prayer, seek to involve the youngsters actively in them and frequently include a dialogue between the celebrant and the children.

In the sermon he first tells them a story from that day's Gospel. Next, he creates for them a picture of the scene. Then he urges his little listeners to make of this a moving, talking picture employing all of their senses to do so. Finally, Father English helps them to get the idea behind this human incident in the life of Jesus. Thus he gives his hearers a story, picture, movie and idea.

In this process the Jesuit priest turns to a variety of visuals for assistance. Once again, the *Directory* encourages such innovations:

> The liturgy of the Mass contains many visual elements, and these should be given great prominence with children. This is especially true of the particular visual elements in the course of the liturgical year, for example, the veneration of the cross, the Easter candle, the lights on the feast

Liturgy of the Word

of the Presentation of the Lord, and the variety of colors and liturgical ornaments (Article 35).

"For the same reason the use of pictures prepared by the children themselves may be useful, for example, to illustrate a homily, to give a visual dimension to the intentions of the general intercessions, or to inspire reflection" (Article 36).

Does all of this bear spiritual fruit? Large crowds at the liturgies regularly over several years say something about the drawing power of his approach.

Comments from adults are likewise quite convincing:

"We used to drag the kids to church. Now they drag us."

"They used to sing pop songs from the radio, now they sing songs from Mass."

12. Praying for Others

I was deeply touched on my initial Marriage Encounter when I received a note indicating about 50 couples at home were praying for me throughout that weekend experience. Moreover, it became clear that those assurances of prayer on my behalf were neither empty promises nor mere token symbols of loving support.

These husbands and wives really prayed—at home, in church, during Mass, before meals, some even at 2:00 or 3:00 in the morning with alarms set for the designated hours.

Such petitions are both helpful and healing. We have the Lord's own example and promise about the power of prayer to aid others in distress. In addition, however, the awareness that a community of believers cares enough to mention your name in prayer has by itself a very healing effect on the hurting person.

We have found that to be the case with the General Intercessions or Prayer of the Faithful at our weekend and weekday Masses. The sick and sorrowing are pleased and encouraged when they hear or learn their situation has been placed in prayer before the entire worshiping congregation.

Petitions like these form an appropriate part of the General Intercessions, but its concerns should reach beyond the immediate needs of a few or of the local area.

Liturgy of the Word

Article 45 of the Missal's General Instruction explains that in the

> prayer of the faithful, the people exercise their priestly function by interceding for all mankind. It is appropriate that this prayer be included in all Masses celebrated with a congregation, so that intercessions may be made for the Church, for civil authorities, for those oppressed by various needs, for all mankind, and for the salvation of the world.

The usual order of petitions to be followed touches on the needs of the Church, then public authorities and the salvation of the world, next, those oppressed by any need and, finally, the local community.

Here are some practical suggestions with regard to the General Intercessions:

* The petitions should include specific and contemporary concerns, not be limited to abstract generalizations. The late-night television news on Friday, the Saturday morning paper and the radio reports will readily provide issues on the minds of that weekend's worshipers.

* Spontaneous petitions from the congregation are normally ineffective for large, Sunday Masses. They tend to be subjective and inaudible.

* The people's response ought to vary, but not too often. In the latter instance, the community's lack of familiarity with the frequently changed phrase will bring an uncomfortable insecurity and result in a weak sung or spoken reply.

* Attractive banners displaying the congregation's response facilitates a strong reply, even when alternated, for example, every month.

* A concluding petition, "For your personal intentions," accompanied by a suitable silent pause, individualizes the General Intercession and has proven very popular in our parish.

* Those who assemble for small-group Masses, as on weekdays, and speak forth on-the-spot petitions need to be reminded occasionally that the Prayer of the Faithful has a worldwide vision. We as a congregation pray not only for our family and friends, but for all mankind.

* Parishioners should every now and then be publicly encouraged to submit the names of persons in need to the parish priests or committee in charge of the General Intercessions. Then when someone has been unfortunately omitted, the responsibility falls on the total community rather than on the human, limited person or persons who prepare the petitions.

13. Announcements and the Parish Bulletin

My predecessor initiated a very wise policy for weekend Masses: he insisted the parish bulletin be distributed after the liturgy, not beforehand.

That procedure avoids or eliminates many problems. Youngsters are not able to make paper airplanes so easily during Mass; adults more readily listen to the homily rather than read through the bulletin; the pews remain relatively free of litter after each Eucharist.

This in no way minimizes the importance or value of that weekly newsletter. Nor does it suggest we spend a lengthy period at Mass giving verbal announcements which already appear in the printed bulletin. Such a practice, unfortunately still prevalent in many churches, really insults the intelligence of worshipers and causes them to disregard the published handout. Why read this piece of paper when its contents have just been proclaimed from the pulpit?

Our experience over five years indicates that people do check the bulletin quite carefully and will respond to its messages with little or no mention of those items from the altar. This enhances the prayerful atmosphere of the liturgy itself and keeps distractions at a minimum. Persons who come to church hoping to hear a message about Jesus Christ the Lord, King and Messiah find frustrating the recitation of tedious announcements about forthcoming meetings or activities.

The Roman Missal rather subtly, it seems to me, makes a similar point. In its section giving the rubrics for the celebration of Mass with a congregation, the General Instruction, article 123, only suggests there may be announcements and places them at the end of Mass before the concluding rite.

This directive states: "If there are any brief announcements, they may be made at this time." Note the "if," the "brief," and the fact the Church locates these messages here rather than before or after the sermon.

An attractive bulletin, interestingly written and full of significant material, serves as one of the strongest communciation vehicles we have in a parish. A few illustrations should prove that point.

* Mention of who will preach next week and on what topic stimulates interest. It also reveals to the people the advance planning which has gone into the Sunday liturgy and homily.

* Listing the scheduled lectors and gift-bearers for the day's Masses helps build a community spirit. "I often wondered who that family was." "So that's the reader's name."

* Reporting the previous weekend's collection and noting any major expenditures fosters trust, shifts the financial burden from the priest's to the congregation's shoulders and is a step toward fiscal accountability.

* Welcoming by name new Christians or parishioners as well as mentioning the sick or deceased deepens the bond linking the parish family together.

Last fall at Holy Family we developed a leaflet, "Holy Family Happenings, 1976-77," distributed after all the Masses during a September weekend. Based on a similar

Liturgy of the Word

publication from another parish, it noted the schedule of activities for the coming year with, among other data, specific dates for all instructions connected with the First Communion, First Penance and Confirmation programs.

Photos taken the previous year of parallel events and a professional layout by an artist-parishioner enhanced the beauty of this program. We hope it will be fixed to refrigerators and remind people of coming events.

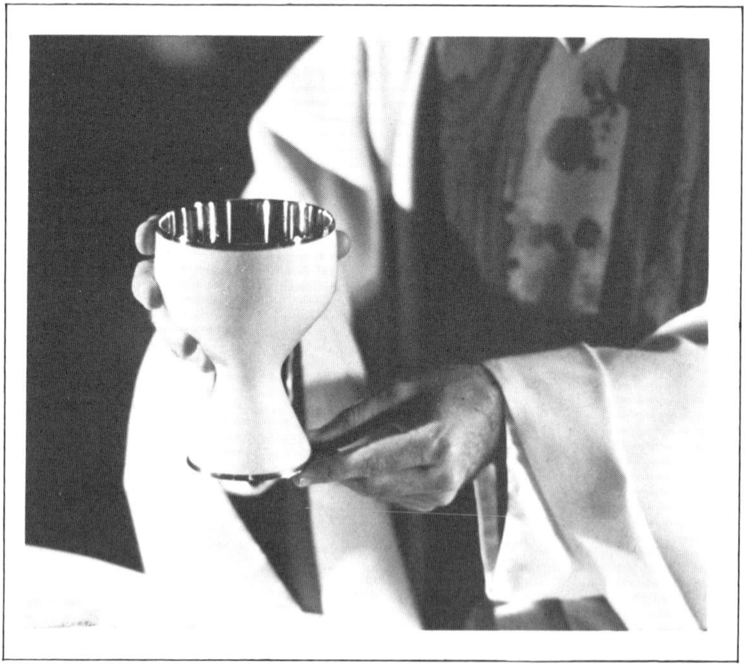

PART III:
Liturgy of the Eucharist

Liturgy of the Eucharist

At the Last Supper Christ instituted the paschal sacrifice and meal. In this meal the sacrifice of the cross is continually made present in the Church when the priest, representing Christ, carries out what the Lord did and handed over to his disciples to do in his memory.

Christ took bread and the cup, gave thanks, broke, and gave to his disciples, saying "Take and eat, this is my body. Take and drink, this is the cup of my blood. Do this in memory of me." The Church has arranged the celebration of the eucharistic liturgy to correspond to these word and actions of Christ:

1) In the preparation of the gifts, bread, wine, and water are brought to the altar, the same elements which Christ used.

2) The eucharistic prayer is the hymn of thanksgiving to God for the whole work of salvation; the offerings become the body and blood of Christ.

3) The breaking of the one bread is a sign of the unity of the faithful, and in communion they receive the body and blood of Christ as the Apostles did from his hands.

—*The Roman Missal,* General Instruction

14. Offering Symbolic Gifts

For 10 months in 1976-77 I served as pastor-in-residence at the North American College, Rome, Italy, a seminary for theological students in their last years of preparation for the priesthood.

One morning I was an hour's drive from the Eternal City, up in the hills of the Frascati wine region near our Holy Father's summer residence. The Jesuit retreat house, "Villa Cavalletti," which overlooks a small Italian town or city named Grottaferrata became my home for three days. During World War II, Field Marshal Kesselring, commander of the German troops in Italy, established his headquarters and residence in this lovely building surrounded by its grapevines, fruit orchards and neatly clipped hedges.

Two dozen seminarians, some from the North American College and others from the American College in Louvain, Belgium, had gathered there for a weeklong spiritual institute. Each day's schedule included a presentation or two by an outside speaker like myself, group discussions, abundant time for reading and reflection, Mass, morning and evening prayers.

Prior to watching a magnificent fireworks display emanating from the festival celebration below us in Grottaferrata, we joined together one night in the main conference room for informal evening prayer.

Several brought candles for the center table so that all participants might sit in semidarkness around the flickering tapers. Following the reading of a scripture passage, some of the students, as requested earlier, placed on the table objects symbolizing major experiences of the day.

Each presenter spoke a spontaneous prayer to the Father explaining the significance of the gift being offered. Some of the symbols were to be expected, others, quite unusual:

* "A pair of glasses which helped me see the beauty of your creation in this gorgeous spot."

* "An apple which symbolizes all the good things of nature you have given to me."

* "A prayer book which has been my constant aid and companion in talking with you today."

* "A pillow representing the great sleep I had today made possible because of the deep peace and contentment I found here."

Bringing forward similar symbolic objects during the presentation of gifts at a eucharistic liturgy can fulfill a similar purpose for the congregation.

The Roman Missal's General Instruction encourages such an offertory procession. Article 49 notes:

> The offerings are then brought forward: it is desirable for the faithful to present the bread and wine which are accepted by the priest or deacon at a suitable place. These are placed on the altar with the accompanying prayers. The rite of carrying up the gifts continues the spiritual value and meaning of the ancient custom when the people brought bread and wine for the liturgy from their homes.

In addition to the bread and wine, this also may be the occasion for bringing up other needed items for the

Liturgy of the Eucharist

Church or poor (the Sunday collection of money or Thanksgiving food for the hungry).

Similarly, for special celebrations certain symbolic gifts like the seminarians' night prayer offerings might be presented. For example:

* At a funeral, several objects which represent the major events or interests of the deceased.

* At a wedding, a few items expressing the couple's love for each other and their hopes for the future.

* At Christmas, toys from the children for the child Jesus which will later be distributed to needy youngsters.

15. The Offertory Procession

I have found while calling at homes of strayed sheep or visiting with persons who have stopped worshiping regularly on Sundays, the most common explanation given for their absence from Mass is this: priests were always preaching about or asking for money.

That objection may, in many or most cases, simply be a rationalization, in effect a kind of cop-out to cover up laziness, indifference, a guilty conscience or lack of faith. But in some instances the clergy have been preoccupied in the pulpit with financial concerns.

We hope, of course, that priests today avoid such an undue emphasis and limit their monetary appeals to once or twice a year spiritual exhortations on the value of generosity in sharing with others.

However, they should not shift to the opposite extreme by removing the collection of a congregation's offerings from the worship service. This conveys the impression that money is evil and unclean, bad and unworthy of the liturgy.

Neither current Church directives nor ancient Christian tradition supports such a view. The present *Roman Missal* in its General Instruction, article 49, speaking of the period after the General Intercessions and before the preparation of bread and wine at the altar, recommends: "This is also the time to bring forward or to collect money or gifts for the poor and the Church. These are to be laid in a suitable place but not on the altar."

Church history, moreover, indicates that the procession of gifts dates to the first Christian centuries. We even find written testimony in the *Ordines Romani* as early as the end of the 7th century that the pope, flanked by assistants, came down toward the people to receive their offerings.

In the beginning, not only bread and wine were brought forward, but also other items destined for use in the church, e.g., oil and candles. From the 11th century on, however, legal tender gradually replaced these specific objects.

Some parishes, in an attempt to minimize distractions at the Eucharist, place baskets near the entrances before Mass. Ushers then merely collect those receptacles after the liturgy begins, combine their contents, and carry them to the altar after the General Intercessions.

We prefer a different and probably more common approach.

The celebrant sits after the Prayer of the Faithful as an ample number of ushers quickly come to the front with the collection baskets. These are then handed from person to person with the usher only supervising the flow from one pew to the next. With the task completed, a family (or the ushers, if the assigned people fail to show) brings forward the bread, wine and money.

This procedure possesses several advantages: it provides a quiet reflection time after the homily with, if feasible, appropriate instrumental or choral background music; it means the celebrant does not proceed with the Mass until after the collection has been finished; it gives parishioners a more active part in the gathering process; it makes the procession a very natural and needed ceremony; it involves a family more intimately in the liturgy.

Fulfilling the function of gift-bearer is an honor, but still a challenge for most families. Being on public display while taking up the offerings and more, when returning to their seats, tends to make our parishioners a bit nervous. When the assigned Sunday nears, it usually calls for haircuts and best dresses and shined shoes, sometimes even the sacrament of Penance for an entire household.

For that reason, we avoid asking people to fulfill that function as they enter the church before Mass or tapping persons in the pews for the task prior to a celebration. This diminishes its significance and can cause discomfort among parishioners.

Instead, a bimonthly list is sent with the date and Mass assigned and each family's phone number. They can then, on their own, make any switches necessary.

16. Simple, but Symbolic, Gestures

Those of us whose attitudes for participation at Mass were formed prior to the Second Vatican Council tended then to place a great emphasis on the offertory rite. We tried at that point to "offer" our lives with its recent ups and downs, successes and failures as the priest "offered" the bread and wine.

There was nothing drastically wrong with such an approach. But the practice did, however, seem to overemphasize this portion of the liturgy. Further, it distracted from the essential sacrifice and oblation of the Church which is performed later at the consecration and the memorial offering immediately afterwards.

The new order of Mass follows a middle course in its revision of the offertory. The rite has not been reduced to a mere preparation of bread and wine with only one prayer, an oration over the gifts at the conclusion. Yet neither has the earlier version with many prayers and a heavy "offering" motif been retained. A look at several portions of this section in the eucharistic liturgy should illustrate that compromise pattern.

* The lengthy, offering prayers which accompanied the elevation of bread and wine have been replaced by short statements of praise. These new texts are based on ancient formulas, probably the very words used for the blessing of bread and wine in Jewish meals during our Lord's time.

> Blessed are you, Lord God of all creation. Through your goodness we have this bread to offer, which earth has given and human hands have made.
>
> It will become for us the bread of life.

A similar one, of course, is employed for the wine. Unfortunately, many celebrants today have on their own adopted a practice of combining the two blessing prayers and elevating the bread and wine together.

* The mixing of a little water with the wine has been preserved because of its extremely ancient tradition. However, the companion prayer is now reduced to the essential words. These ask that what began with the Incarnation (God become man) may now be fulfilled in this sacrament. The formula also requests that we might share in the divinity of him, Jesus, who became man for us.

St. Cyprian, in the third century, saw in this mingling of the water and wine a clear indication that the sacrifice of Christ also embraces the Christian people. To quote from the great liturgical scholar, Jesuit Father Josef Jungmann, summarizing Cyprian's thought:

> As Christ has borne our sins by his sufferings, so too in this sacrifice the people are joined to Christ just as inseparably as the water to the wine, and thus are included in the gifts offered up.

Hence, the water disappearing into and linked inseparably with the wine symbolizes several mysteries of our faith: the intimate union of God and man achieved through Christ's coming into the world; the marvelous share in Jesus' divinity we are offered through grace; the close link between ourselves and the Lord's sacrifice.

Liturgy of the Eucharist

* The washing of the celebrant's hands had a very pragmatic function in early centuries. They would have been soiled by his receiving and disposing of the bread, wine, oil, candles and other gifts of the people brought forward following the homily. In our day this normally is not the case. Nevertheless, the Church retains the gesture due to both its ancient nature and symbolic value.

The General Instruction in article 52 notes: "The priest washes his hands as an expression of his desire for inward purification."

It is regrettable how often either that symbolic cleansing has been omitted by the priest or performed almost invisibly. The washing of hands as a symbol needs little explanation and, accomplished with a large pitcher and basin in the clear view of the congregation, can be effective in an era bereft of many religious signs.

* Article 51 reads: "The gifts on the altar and the altar itself may be incensed. This is a symbol of the Church's offering and prayer going up to God. Afterwards the deacon or other minister may incense the priest and the people."

One of our students here commented on how incensation of the people emphasizes their Christian dignity. He observed that as a lay person sitting in the pews before his entrance into the seminary.

17. An Ancient but Current Prayer

From the roof of our North American College, six floors up, we have a superb panoramic view of Rome. In fact, the rector, Msgr. Harold Darcy, a native of Newark, New Jersey, believes one can see better from here than even from the top of St. Peter's because we are able also to study the great dome of that basilica which the person there obviously cannot do.

Looking out over the city gave me a sensation of being touched by the past, the present, and the future.

In Rome, the past certainly stands out before your eyes. Everywhere you pass pre-Christian ruins from thick walls and still-standing gates to aqueducts and amphitheaters. The location of chariot races like the one filmed in *Ben-Hur* is clearly visible and but a stone's throw away as you drive by in a small Fiat.

You also capture the martyr atmosphere of those first Christian centuries. Carved in Latin letters on an upper side of our building is this phrase which really says it all: "O happy Rome, you have been consecrated by the glorious blood of your two leaders."

The catacombs and other churches remind us that many Christians in every age have followed the footsteps of St. Peter and St. Paul by pouring out their lives for the sake of Jesus.

St. Peter's itself, but a five-minute walk down the hill from the college, brings us through many past centuries into the present and onto the future. On Sundays, for example, Pope Paul will often canonize a saint, declaring that this holy servant of God who labored perhaps only a generation or so ago, now enjoys the vision of our Father in heaven and intercedes for us.

Holy Mass similarly links together the past, present and future. In the *Constitution of the Sacred Liturgy,* article 47 reminds us:

> At the Last Supper, on the night he was betrayed, our Savior instituted the eucharistic sacrifice of his Body and Blood. This he did in order to perpetuate the sacrifice of the Cross throughout the ages until he should come again, so to entrust to his beloved spouse, the Church, a memorial of his death and resurrection: a sacrament of love, a sign of unity, a bond of charity, a paschal banquet in which Christ is consumed, the mind is filled with grace, and a pledge of future glory is given to us.

The eucharistic prayer through which we celebrate this sacrifice likewise contains elements which are both old and new.

The Sanctus, for example, was added at a very early stage in the development of Mass. The inspiration behind that acclamation came from the Old Testament prophet Isaiah (6:3) who had a vision of the Lord and heard Seraphim crying out: "Holy, holy, is the Lord of hosts. . . . All the earth is filled with his glory."

The Benedictus, which follows immediately, looks beyond and above us. That song of praise takes its inspiration and origin from sections of the Book of Revelation or Apocalypse like this one in 5:13: "To the one seated on the throne, and to the Lamb, be praise and honor, glory and might, forever and ever."

Eucharistic prayer II, made public with two others in 1968, has roots in the very ancient past. It is substantially the text Hippolytus of Rome wrote down around the year 215.

However, not all the developments or additions in our eucharistic prayer formula throughout the centuries were positive and beneficial. Thus, to illustrate, the silent canon with prayers recited only by the priest and in a subdued tone complicated the liturgy's structure and reduced the people's participation.

The Council Fathers understood this. Yet they were most careful to insist that the Mass reforms reflect accurately our past and ancient tradition. Article 50, as a consequence, reads:

> The rite of the Mass is to be revised in such a way that the intrinsic nature and purpose of its several parts, as well as the connection between them, may be more clearly manifested, and that devout and active participation by the faithful may be more easily achieved.
>
> For this purpose the rites are to be simplified, due care being taken to preserve their substances. Parts which with the passage of time came to be duplicated, or were added with little advantage, are to be omitted. Other parts which suffered loss through accidents of history are to be restored to the vigor they had in the days of the holy Fathers as may seem useful or necessary.

18. Elements of the Eucharistic Prayer

This essay, slightly technical, will outline the chief elements of a Eucharistic Prayer. Presently in the Roman rite we have nine available for use, with additional ones now being composed and prepared for possible Vatican approval.

Each text, however, basically incorporates all the elements noted below.

* *Thanksgiving.* The Eastern rite Churches include in their altar books 75 or more canons or Eucharistic Prayers. Each one has its own preface or invitation to thanksgiving.

The Roman liturgy, on the other hand, supplies celebrants with but a few as noted above. However, the Missal offers to them a rich choice of many prefaces for use with one or another of the nine Eucharistic Prayers. That preface situates the day's celebration, points out the reason why at this moment, in this place, we render to God the Father our praise and thanksgiving. What the Eastern rite does through an entire Eucharistic Prayer, the Roman liturgy accomplishes in the preface.

* *Acclamations.* There are three which the people sing or recite: the Sanctus or Holy, Holy, Holy Lord, the Memorial Acclamation after the Consecration, and the "Amen" at the doxology's conclusion.

All of these belong to the congregation and for that reason the music during those acclamations should be sung at least in part by the people. A long, choir-only Sanctus, regardless of how magnificent, violates these principles and reduces the congregation to mute spectators.

Similarly, the concluding doxology, "Through him, with him, in him . . . ," should be proclaimed by the celebrant alone or with the other priests, if it is a concelebration. That procedure invites the congregation to respond in a loud, united, stirring Amen, a word here signifying affirmation or agreement with the priest's statements of faith.

In circumstances where the congregation regrettably joins the celebrant in this "Through him . . ." doxology, their Amen loses its meaning and normally also lacks power or volume.

* *Epiclesis.* This theological term denotes a calling forth of the Holy Spirit upon the gifts presented and the people participating. To quote the General Instruction, number 55c:

"In special invocations the Church calls on God's power and asks that the gifts offered by men may be consecrated, that is, become the body and blood of Christ and that the victim may become a source of salvation for those who are to share in communion."

Normally, the first invocation occurs before the Consecration and the second, afterwards.

* *Narrative of the institution and Consecration.* Again the Missal summarizes this portion of the Eucharistic Prayer.

"In the words and actions of Christ, the sacrifice he instituted at the Last Supper is celebrated, when under the appearances of bread and wine he offered his body and blood, gave them to his Apostles to eat and drink, and

Liturgy of the Eucharist

commanded them to carry on this mystery."

The time, however, for breaking the host or bread is not now, but later during the Lamb of God.

* *Memorial.* The proper term, "Anamnesis," simply means a remembering, and in this portion the Church "keeps his memorial by recalling especially his passion, resurrection and ascension." It occurs, of course, immediately after the Consecration.

* *Offering.* The whole Church and the Church here and now assembled offer the victim to the Father in the Holy Spirit.

"The Church's intention is that the faithful not only offer the spotless victim, but also learn to offer themselves and daily to be drawn into ever more perfect union, through Christ the Mediator, with the Father and with each other, so that at last God may be all in all."

* *Intercessions.* We are reminded through these petitions for the living and the dead that Mass is celebrated in communion with the whole Church in heaven and on earth.

19. Our Holy Father and the Mass

Mention the word "pope" or the name Pope Paul VI to certain persons, including some Roman Catholics, and you can immediately sense a feeling of reserve, displeasure, even hostility come over them.

For those people the pope is a distant figure dressed in white, that man who rules with unquestioned authority a mammoth, cold, institutional, highly organized Church, the individual behind those Vatican statements which seem so out of touch with today's society.

Here in Rome we look at Pope Paul from a different viewpoint, an approach reflected in the title most often used when speaking about him: our Holy Father. This vision of Pope Paul sees him as the universal man of prayer, a sensitive, singular individual who carries the burdens and joys of the entire world, of every nation in his heart.

That universality and humanness become very evident in the weekly papal audiences. They are held on Wednesday mornings at 11:00 in the plain, spacious, but extremely functional hall constructed specifically for these gatherings.

I sat for a September audience in the glass-enclosed press area, a section equipped with closed-circuit television. This marvelous vantage point above the 7,000 participants and at one side of the auditorium enabled me to see everything and hear each word.

Liturgy of the Eucharist

Before the Holy Father arrived, commentators described in several languages the traditional procedure Pope Paul would follow during his audience: the sign of the cross, a brief religious message, introduction of the bishops present, acknowledgment of special groups from many nations, the Our Father (in Latin) and a final blessing.

The universal quality of both the sign of the cross and the sung "Pater Noster" strikes an observer at once. So, too, however, does the introduction of a dozen bishops who are in Rome on business or pilgrimage. They came, for example, from such places as Canada, Australia, Poland, Italy and Africa, including a native prelate from that down-under continent. Those in the audience hall proper likewise had traveled to Rome for this audience from every corner of the earth.

Pope Paul spoke and acted indeed as a holy, spiritual, caring father. He talked about the needs of people today, not only their bodily or material demands, but their spiritual requirements as well.

Then the Holy Father introduced the various groups of pilgrims, often interjecting a comment of encouragement or a word of concern.

After the final blessing, Pope Paul moved slowly about to greet individually a few persons or clusters of participants. He gave a warm embrace to a retired Lutheran bishop from Sweden; showed special affection for the visiting priests from Milan (his episcopal see before election as pope); waved with enthusiasm to the numerous newlyweds assembled in their normal spot near the right front section of the hall.

Often during the audience our Holy Father extended his particular blessing to the elderly, the infirm and the children. In what was for me the most moving portion of the morning, Pope Paul put those words into practice at the conclusion of the hour-and-a-half event.

A pilgrimage of invalids from Boston were summoned forward by the Pope when he had completed the formal portion of the program. An older woman, carried in a wheelchair to the Holy Father, received his individual blessing. Then a man bearing in his arms a young son without any arms stepped up. Pope Paul kissed the child, embraced the father and blessed them both.

This is the man we pray for at every Mass during the Eucharistic Prayer. We speak to God on his behalf, worship in union with him and call him to mind at the important part of the liturgy.

One makes that prayer and remembrance differently after a papal audience. We begin to pray with and for a holy man, a caring person, a father of many.

20. Communion of Saints

When heavyset, always smiling and constantly chuckling Andy Lukach left his Wilkes-Barre, Pennsylvania, home three summers ago, there was neither joy in his heart nor radiance upon his face.

This young man in his early 20's faced a 5,000-mile trip across the Atlantic, four years of seminary training in a foreign country, and community life with a group of strangers, all American, but from 44 states and 85 dioceses. The prospect of entering first theology at the North American College here in Rome certainly excited and challenged him. Yet anxiety about the unknown, as well as the pain of separation from loved ones, dampened his enthusiasm.

At that time Andy carried an additional burden which caused lines of sadness in his usually cheerful face and a pensive silence in his normally bubbling personality. A few days before departure Mrs. Lukach had died of cancer.

Last fall Andy received a telephone message from the United States around 6:00 a.m. His father had died suddenly, leaving Andy and his younger brother the only surviving members of that family.

A heaviness came over both faculty and students as word of this popular seminarian's newest cross filtered that day throughout the college community. We shared his pain.

The instructors learned of it during our regular staff meeting. We went to the front door hoping to give him our group support before his trip to the airport, but he had already left.

A notice on the bulletin board announced the news and listed his home address. The next day's mailbox contained many cards and aerograms addressed to him with consoling messages from his brother Christians, the N.A.C. faculty and students.

That night during our community Mass, a concelebrating priest prayed from the third Eucharistic Prayer:

> Remember John Lukach.
> In baptism he died with Christ:
> may he also share his resurrection,
> when Christ will raise our mortal bodies
> and make them like his own in glory.
> Welcome into your Kingdom our departed brothers
>   and sisters,
> and all who have left this world in your friendship.
> There we hope to share in your glory
> when every tear will be wiped away.
> On that day we shall see you, our God, as you are.
> We shall become like you and praise you
> for ever through Christ our Lord,
> from whom all good things come.

Andy's suffering and his father's death brought home a bit more clearly to us that doctrine we profess called the communion of saints. As a recent Vatican document explains the dogma:

> It means that the life of each individual son of God is joined in Christ and through Christ by a wonderful link to the life of all his other Christian brethren. Together they form the supernatural unity of Christ's mystical Body so that, as it were, a single mystical person is formed (*Apostolic Constitution on the Revision of Indulgences,* January 1, 1967).

Liturgy of the Eucharist

At every Mass in the Eucharistic Prayer we put this doctrine into practice through the intercessions. These "make it clear that the eucharist is celebrated in communion with the whole Church of heaven and earth, and that the offering is made for the Church and all its members, living and dead, who are called to share in the salvation and redemption acquired by the body and blood of Christ" (*The Roman Missal*'s General Instruction, article 55g).

A comforting thought: In the Eucharist we not only pray for separated loved ones, living and deceased, but are united with them in the Lord's body and blood.

21. The Coming of the Spirit

Immediately before what we commonly call the Consecration of Mass, the celebrant extends both hands over the bread and cup. With palms thus outstretched, he prays in phrases like these taken from the second Eucharistic Prayer:

> Let your Spirit come upon these gifts to make
>   them holy,
> so that they may become for us
> the body and blood of our Lord, Jesus Christ.

During the recitation of that invocation directed toward the Holy Spirit, the priest also traces a cross over the host and chalice.

Following the institutional narrative or Consecration, the celebrant once again invokes the Holy Spirit in words similar to the ones below from the third Eucharistic Prayer:

> Grant that we, who are nourished by his body
>   and blood,
> may be filled with his Holy Spirit,
> and become one body, one spirit in Christ.

These two portions of the Eucharistic Prayer form the "epiclesis," a calling forth of the Holy Spirit into our midst. The Roman Missal explains its function:

> "In special invocations the Church calls on God's power and asks that the gifts offered by men may be con-

Liturgy of the Eucharist

secrated, that is, become the body and blood of Christ and that the victim may become a source of salvation for those who are to share in communion" (General Instruction, article 55c).

Those simple gestures of extended hands and sign of the cross over the gifts have considerable impact upon a congregation now that the priest performs them in view of the people. A few years ago, concealed from the worshipers, they were a signal for the server to ring the warning bell. It was his serious responsibility to catch that gesture, even if he had to peer around the celebrant's back for a better look. How many altar boys drew an impatient glance or sharp remark from the priest when they missed this gesture! Today, however, the congregation is at that point silent and observant, making the outstretched hands a more significant sign and symbol.

In the first Christian centuries the priest normally bowed during this prayer. However, from the close of the Middle Ages onward instead the hands were extended, coupled later with a sign of the cross. For the balance of this chapter I would like to discuss those two gestures.

* At the start, the outstretched hands apparently formed a mere pointing gesture, indicating what were the gifts being offered to God.

* Later a symbolic or interpretative meaning tended to be added to the extension of hands. These generally referred the gesture back to Old Testament practices and sacrifices.

For example, in Leviticus we read of burnt sacrifices or holocausts. "To find favor with the Lord, he shall bring it to the entrance of the meeting tent, and there lay his hand on the head of the holocaust" (1:3-4).

This Old Testament book refers similarly to peace offerings. "If someone is presenting a peace offering . . . he shall lay his hand on the head of his offering" (3:1-2).

Leviticus also describes sin offerings. "Having laid his hands on its head, he shall slaughter the goat as a sin offering before the Lord . . ." (4:24).

Some saw a link here between Christ the victim on the altar who takes upon himself our sins and the old covenant scapegoat who assumed the sins of the Jewish people and was led off into the wilderness.

On the Day of Atonement, Aaron was commanded to

> bring forward the live goat. Laying both hands on its head, he shall confess over it all the sinful faults and transgressions of the Israelites, and so put them on the goat's head. He shall then have it led into the desert by an attendant. Since the goat is to carry off their iniquities to an isolated region, it must be sent away into the desert (16:20-22).

In that approach, Jesus becomes our scapegoat and through these outstretched hands we place our guilt and sins upon him.

* Finally, many saw in this gesture a blessing given to the bread and wine. This would be similar to the benediction bestowed by a priest on some object or by the newly ordained on a person kneeling before him.

For the first 1,000 years in the Church, blessings were customarily made through the laying on of hands. Gradually, however, the sign of the cross superseded that gesture for benedictions. The present rite obviously combines both elements.

Whatever may be those added, symbolic meanings, the main thrust of that extension of hands over the gifts at Mass in our day is a petition asking, "Father, may this Holy Spirit sanctify these offerings" (Eucharistic Prayer IV).

22. The Lord's Prayer

Two mountains, the first smaller than the second, each with an ascending and descending slope.

We can, in a simplified view of the Mass, break down its overall structure into two such movements.

Throughout that initial, lesser mountain, called the Liturgy of the Word, our attention centers around the bible and the pulpit from which the spoken message comes to us.

During this section of Mass, we speak to God (e.g., the Penitential Rite, Gloria, opening prayer), then the Lord speaks to us (e.g., scriptural proclamations and homily). Hence, we visualize these as ascending and descending slopes.

Throughout that second, greater mountain, called the Liturgy of the Eucharist, our attention centers around the gifts, offered or received, and the altar upon which these items rest.

During this section of Mass, we give to God (the bread, wine, money, ourselves, Christ present under the consecrated species) and then the Lord gives to us (Jesus' body and blood in Communion). Once again, we picture these as ascending and descending slopes.

The Lord's Prayer forms a turning point in that second, larger mountain and begins the downward movement in which God gives himself to us. In the more technical words of the Roman Missal's General Instruction:

"Since the eucharistic celebration is the paschal meal, in accord with his command, the body and blood should be received as spiritual food by the faithful who are properly disposed. This is the purpose of the breaking of the bread and the other preparatory rites which lead directly to the communion of the people" (Article 56).

Here are a few comments or explanatory notes about the Lord's Prayer.

* The celebrant introduces this prayer with a few phrases of his own or from the Missal to dispose us more suitably for its recitation or singing. It would be a bold or daring presumption to call God one's Father without some such preliminaries.

* The prayer has a value all its own simply because Jesus taught us the words (see Matthew 6:9-13; Luke 11:2-4). However, the text likewise smoothly links together the immediately preceding upward motion and the now downward movement.

The first portion speaks to our Father about the kingdom of God and its coming: "Our Father, who art in heaven, hallowed be thy name: thy kingdom come, thy will be done on earth as it is in heaven."

The second section still addresses the Father, but about our needs: "Give us this day our daily bread; and forgive us our trespasses as we forgive those who trespass against us; and lead us not into temptation, but deliver us from evil."

* The daily bread mentioned has been understood as far back as the time of St. Ambrose to include not only the bread for our bodies which we obviously require, but also the food for our hearts or souls which is equally essential.

Liturgy of the Eucharist

* Christians in the early centuries likewise stressed the words, "Forgive us our trespasses as we forgive those who trespass against us." In St. Augustine's community at Hippo, all present struck their breasts during these phrases.

The revised *Roman Missal* makes note of both points when it comments on the Lord's Prayer:

"This is a petition both for daily food, which for Christians means also the eucharistic bread, and for forgiveness from sin, so that what is holy may be given to those who are holy" (Article 56a).

* The section following the Our Father's conclusion is termed the embolism, or insertion, which expands upon the last phrase, "deliver us from evil."

* This embolism concludes with the doxology, "For the Kingdom, the power, and the glory are yours now and forever." Quite similar to what one might call the Protestant ending of the Lord's Prayer, it represents an adaptation of the verse which occurs in some (not all, or even most) ancient manuscripts as a part of Matthew's account of the Our Father.

* To express a sense of unity before our common Father, worshipers in small groups today occasionally will join hands for the Lord's Prayer. Moreover, those in the charismatic movement are inclined to raise their arms toward heaven as they say or sing this most ancient of prayers.

23. The Sign of Peace

John and Sharon no longer come to Mass at Holy Family. Their families do and they did until a few months after their marriage.

At that time, however, the young wife, rather shy and somewhat timid, experienced a painful rejection one Saturday night at the Eucharist. During the sign of peace, she turned with some hesitation to a neighbor and offered her hand and cautious smile as a gesture of Christian love. The individual frowned, then faced in the opposite direction.

Sharon, deeply hurt by this negative personal response, also judged that everyone in the church saw the incident and she felt greatly embarrassed.

The next week John joined his wife for Mass. At the sign of peace on this occasion both experienced similar unfortunate rejections. It was more than they wished to endure. Soon John and Sharon joined another parish, one which had not yet introduced the gesture of reconciliation.

I doubt if that event would repeat itself today. A recent national survey investigating contemporary religious attitudes indicates that roughly 75 percent of Roman Catholics now accept the sign of peace. Moreover, most parishes have implemented the following directions of the *Roman Missal:*

Liturgy of the Eucharist

"Rite of peace: before they share in the same bread, the people express their love for one another and beg for peace and unity in the Church and with all mankind" (General Instruction, Article 56b).

The gesture of peace is not truly an innovation in the liturgy, but, instead, the reintroduction of a practice which has its roots in early Christian tradition and even existed before the time of Jesus.

Jews greeted one another with "Shalom," a kindly wish that all of God's blessings might come upon the neighbor. We see that illustrated in a negative manner during the incident at Simon's house with our Lord and the penitent woman who washed his feet.

Christ criticized his host: "You gave me no kiss, but she has been covering my feet with kisses ever since I came in" (Lk 7:45). That "kiss" was the Shalom greeting customarily bestowed upon a guest invited for a meal.

Throughout the first Christian centuries, this sign of peace occurred at the conclusion of the homily and the Liturgy of the Word. It was considered a seal of approval and affirmation, an acceptance of the word proclaimed.

Furthermore, at that position, just prior to the presentation of gifts, it linked naturally with these words of Matthew:

"So then, if you are bringing your offering to the altar and there remember that your brother has something against you, leave your offering there before the altar, go and be reconciled with your brother first, and then come back and present your offering" (Mt 5:23-24).

Nevertheless, in a century or two the pattern changed and the gesture of reconciliation was moved to its present location, after the Our Father and before Holy Communion.

The sign of peace exchanged following the Lord's Prayer translates one of its petitions into specific practice.

"Forgive us our trespasses as we forgive those who trespass against us." We must be willing to forgive and be reconciled with our neighbor, if we hope to receive personal forgiveness from God.

The gesture of peace also serves as a preparation for Communion. We share together at the altar the one body and the one blood of Christ. It is hardly fitting that individuals receive the Lord of love and forgiveness who are not reconciled, who bear bitterness in their hearts, who presently refuse to love or forgive some person or persons. Offering a sign of reconciliation to those around us in Church can help remove those poisonous attitudes and make our inner selves more suitable for reception of the Eucharistic Jesus.

For that action to achieve this purpose, we need to see beyond the actual worshipers next to us in the pew. Those individuals represent every human who has touched our lives, including the ones who have in any way hurt us. When we say, "Peace be with you," we really should mean, "I wish to be at peace with you and all persons, especially those against whom I hold any hard feelings."

Such an understandably difficult gesture will nevertheless free our hearts and allow us to approach the Lord's table in peace.

24. The Breaking of Bread

A dozen women in Holy Family Parish belong to a volunteer group we call the "altar-bread bakers." Each week, according to a schedule developed and supervised by the rectory housekeeper, Lena Crisafulle, one of these ladies bakes enough bread to carry us through the Sunday liturgies and for the days which follow.

These loaves are not, however, the thin, white, perfectly round hosts customary for many years in most Catholic churches. Prepared according to the recipe used in a midwest Benedictine monastery, they have instead a brownish color and more substance, while still retaining a circular shape and unleavened character.

Each loaf of this bread is about one half inch thick and approximately six inches in diameter. We break it during the Lamb of God into about 25 to 30 pieces for distribution to communicants. The number of loaves used depends on the particular Mass and the expected number of worshipers (two for 7:00; three for 8:30; five or six for 9:45 and 11:15).

In addition, we occasionally consecrate and reserve in the tabernacle a quantity of the older-style white wafers to care for the overflow of communicants and to provide for those persons who strongly object to this innovation. By simply waiting until near the end of the Communion procedure, they normally receive the thin hosts because we have by then exhausted the supply of "brown" altar breads.

The present practice now meets with fairly broad-based approval in the parish. At the beginning five years ago, on the contrary, we encountered significant opposition and met with difficulties in developing breads which were suitable.

Patient preaching and teaching plus a gentle approach giving to objectors the alternative described above gradually dissolved most of the hostility. Equally patient experimentation with various recipes and methods has led us to the current generally acceptable product.

Our efforts in this area stemmed from the following directive from the revised *Roman Missal:*

> The nature of the sign demands that the material for the eucharistic celebration appear as actual food. The eucharistic bread, even though unleavened and traditional in form, should therefore be made in such a way that the priest can break it and distribute the parts to at least some of the faithful. When the number of communicants is large or other pastoral needs require it, small hosts may be used. The gesture of the breaking of the bread, as the eucharist was called in apostolic times, will more clearly show the eucharist as a sign of unity and charity, since the one bread is being distributed among the members of one family (Article 283).

These new altar breads, then, are not really so much an innovation as a restoration of what was done in the early Christian centuries.

The Missal nevertheless cautions parish leaders: "Care must be taken that the elements be kept in good condition, so that the wine does not sour or the bread spoil or become too hard to be easily broken" (Article 285).

Liturgy of the Eucharist

An Instruction from Rome in 1970 gave more further guidelines about these altar breads: "Though the nature of the sign demands that this bread appear as actual food which can be broken and shared among brothers, it must always be made in the traditional form. . . ."

> The necessity for the sign to be genuine applies more to the colour, taste and texture of the bread than to its shape. Out of reverence for the sacrament, every care and attention should be used in preparing the altar bread. It should be easy to break and should not be unpleasant for the faithful to eat. Bread which tastes of uncooked flour, or which becomes dry and inedible too quickly, must never be used" (Third Instruction on the Correct Implementation of the Sacred Liturgy, article 5).

These altar breads do make it clear that Holy Communion is eating the Lord's Body. They also better remind us of St. Paul's words to the Corinthians: "Because the loaf of bread is one, we, many though we are, are one body, for we all partake of the one loaf" (1 Cor 10:17).

They also, however, give these women, all housewives, a greater sense of belonging to the parish and to the Eucharist. Their married and home lives enter through these loaves into the Mass itself.

25. The Risen Lamb of God

It takes about 60 seconds at our parish to break up the altar breads in preparation for Holy Communion. At the later Masses with fuller congregations, the celebrant, another priest and two lay ministers of the Eucharist stand in clear view of the people and divide the consecrated loaves into smaller particles.

During this process the choir and congregation unite in singing the Agnus Dei or Lamb of God. A rubric in the Roman Missal indicates that the "hymn may be repeated until the breaking of the bread is finished, but the last phrase is always: 'grant us peace.'"

In addition to making clearer the truth that we eat the bread of heaven in Communion, this breaking of the bread or "fractio panis" underscores the unity between celebrant and congregation. Ideally, the priest and people eat of the same loaf, consecrated earlier as one larger whole and now divided into many smaller portions.

That same concept of closeness or oneness between the leader of worship and his fellow Christian believers is stressed a moment further on when everyone, including the priest, recites together: "Lord, I am not worthy to receive you, but only say the word and I shall be healed."

In the hymn or song, "Lamb of God," we call upon or invoke Christ the Savior directly to forgive and shower loving kindness upon us. It points to the past, the present and the future.

Liturgy of the Eucharist

First of all, in the rich scriptural tradition of the Church, we recall the sacrifice of Jesus on the cross, pouring out his blood as a victim, the perfect victim for our sins. Our Lord is the new lamb, even more immaculate than the spotless Old Testament animal whose blood splattered over doorposts in Jewish homes brought deliverance from slavery in Egypt.

The hymn also speaks or sings to Christ the Lamb here and now truly present in our midst as we prepare to receive in a few minutes his body and blood in Communion.

This Lamb of God hymn of praise and petition, finally, looks to the future, our heavenly banquet. That forward glance is made clearer as the priest, following the Lamb of God and a private prayer, elevates the host and says:

> This is the Lamb of God
> who takes away the sins of the World.
> Happy are those who are called to this supper.

The last sentence refers to the Book of Revelation (19:9): "The angel then said to me: 'Write this down: Happy are they who have been invited to the wedding feast of the Lamb.'"

A growing number of celebrants today have developed an unfortunate custom of replacing "they" with "we" and of making other adaptations in this sentence. While not a major issue, such a modification ignores and causes to be lost the very subtle but rich biblical and futuristic content of this acclamation to Christ the Lamb. It likewise unconsciously becomes a more presumptuous declaration and overlooks the mystery of God's call.

While the Lamb of God is being chanted or recited, the priest drops a small particle of the consecrated bread into the cup saying quietly:

> May this mingling of the body and blood of our Lord Jesus Christ
> bring eternal life to us who receive it.

Some would see in that gesture a reunification symbol similar to the separation sign at the institutional narrative. According to this view, the distinct consecration of the bread and wine represents to us the ugly division of Jesus' body and blood on Calvary; the mingling of the two elements now thus speaks to us of the glorious resurrection when Christ's body and blood were reunited, never again to be parted.

However the validity of this approach, the important truth is that we worship the Risen Lord on our altars. Centuries ago, our Lady surely joined with those earliest Christians in celebrating the first eucharistic liturgies. Consequently she, like us, believed in and received her Resurrected Son at those primitive Masses.

As a final preparation for that most important reception of the Lord, the priest prays quietly one of two alternative prayers. The Church indicates these are private words for the celebrant, although once again some priests tend to overlook that rubric and proclaim these in a loud fashion.

In the congregation this should, instead, give them a moment or two of quiet, so they can pray in silence before meeting Christ in the Eucharist.

26. Communion in the Hand and from the Cup

In about a decade two procedures in the Church, practically unheard of in the memory of most American Roman Catholics, have become commonplace throughout the world and in the United States: Communion in the hand and from the cup.

As of this writing bishops' conferences in over 40 nations have approved the optional reception of the Eucharist within the hand and the Holy See has granted permission for that practice. The hierarchy in our own country has not yet endorsed Communion in the hand, but those in such neighboring or closely related places like Canada and England have authorized the procedure within recent years.

This means visitors to the United States tend to bring the custom with them and travelers from here to those lands observe the practice.

The frequently acrimonious debates for and against Communion in the hand seem totally out of proportion to the issue itself. Whether we receive the Lord on our tongue or within the palm appears relatively unimportant. What matters is the faith with which we approach the Lord's table and the reverence displayed toward the Eucharist when receiving it.

Even when approved by a national hierarchy, every communicant still enjoys the option of receiving Christ upon his or her tongue. When properly implemented in a parish, those who come forward for Communion either extend their tongues or their hands. In the second option, the palms should be joined facing upward to form a suitable throne for the eucharistic particle. The communicant at that point or after stepping aside then reverently consumes the host.

The basic reasons behind Communion in the hand are: its ancient tradition (this was the standard practice for the first nine centuries), the fundamental Christian dignity of the whole human body (hand as well as tongue), greater ease in distributing the larger particles of more substantial altar breads, and added active participation by the communicant.

Communion from the cup or under both kinds has been extended as a more frequent practice throughout the universal Church. Unlike Communion in the hand, its authorization was not left to the episcopal conference of each country, but specifically provided for in the new Roman Missal. The extent of implementation, however, depended on the national hierarchy and the local bishop.

In the United States, the National Conference of Catholic Bishops approved such an extensive list of suitable situations for Communion under both kinds that we can say, in summary, the practice is permissible whenever it would prove pastorally possible and spiritually beneficial.

The guidelines encourage, as the preferred method, drinking our Lord's Precious Blood from the cup itself. Jesus' words, "Take and drink" or "He who eats my flesh and drinks my blood . . . ," are more clearly fulfilled and understood in this procedure.

However, in large gatherings with insufficient cups or ministers, the process of Communion under both kinds by intinction frequently serves as the most effective means of distribution. The priest or minister in this circumstance simply dips a host into the cup and places it on the communicant's tongue. Obviously in such a procedure the moistened particle should not be placed in the hand, nor are the larger, thicker pieces of altar breads very convenient. Intinction also becomes a very viable alternative when communicants are afflicted with colds or other contagious diseases.

When introducing Communion from the cup, parishioners should be taught, again, that this is the reintroduction of a practice which was the standard procedure for the first dozen centuries. Moreover, the congregation ought to hear these words of the Roman Missal:

"They should first be reminded that, according to Catholic faith, they receive the whole Christ and the genuine sacrament when they participate in the sacrament even under one kind and that they are not thus deprived of any grace necessary for salvation" (Article 241).

No one should be forced into Communion from the cup or feel uncomfortable about not receiving under both kinds.

27. Alone or Together

Tonight I will concelebrate our evening eucharistic liturgy with perhaps a half dozen other members of the faculty of the North American College in Rome. Unless needed for assistance with the cup, I will simply return to my place following Communion and sit or kneel until all have received the Lord.

In my school days throughout the 1940's and 50's this part of Mass was an intensely personal, sacred period for me. I thus imitated the practice of other Roman Catholics who, during those pre-Vatican II years, would walk back to their pews after Communion, normally bury head in hands and then pour out to the Risen Jesus residing in their hearts very intimate words or concerns.

After Mass we also sometimes remained for a period of private thanksgiving, although seldom fulfilling the dictates of St. Alphonsus Liguori who encouraged "at least a half hour" of such prayer.

Official and unofficial liturgical reforms before and after the Second Vatican Council began to stress the communal or social dimensions of the Eucharist. Holy Communion was not, in this approach, so much my private meeting with Jesus, as a union with brother and sister Christians around the table of the Lord.

To emphasize and deepen this bond, we often sang together during the distribution of the Eucharist. Moreover, leaders reminded us that the Mass itself was the greatest thanksgiving prayer we possess. As a consequence, private "giving thanks" during or after the liturgy seemed to lose popularity and even appeared suspect.

While sitting or kneeling in the pew now after Communion I experience mixed feelings when the music group initiates an appropriate hymn or song. Part of me wishes to join in the community singing; another part, perhaps the product of those formative years, yearns for a few moments of quiet for that personal conversation with the eucharistic Lord. I am sure many Catholics today share similar conflicting desires.

The revised missal speaks to both of these concerns. It first comments on congregational singing at that moment:

"The song during the communion of the priest and people expresses the spiritual union of the communicants who join their voices in a single song, shows the joy of all, and makes the communion procession an act of brotherhood. This song begins when the priest receives communion and continues as long as convenient" (Article 56i).

The text likewise provides for a period of quiet prayer or suitable thanksgiving:

"After communion, the priest and people may spend some time in silent prayer. If desired, a hymn, psalm, or other song of praise may be sung by the entire congregation" (Article 56j).

At Holy Family Parish we have found two practices very effective during this interlude following Communion.

The first is a choral or instrumental melody which in some way underscores the theme of that day's liturgy and homily. This creates an atmosphere that facilitates private prayer and reflection while reinforcing the dominant idea expressed in the celebration.

The second is a minihomily by the celebrant after the brief period of personal silent prayer. In a few sentences he summarizes the major thrust of the sermon itself. Then, after a momentary hesitation and with a change in his tone of voice, he makes one or two announcements about matters of substance. For example:

"We should like to remind you that Thursday is the Feast of All Saints, a holy day of obligation. Please check the bulletin for the schedule of Masses as well as the hour for the sacrament of Penance on Wednesday."

"Today is our monthly social hour and we invite you downstairs after Mass for coffee, cake and conversation."

"Have a good week. We hope to see you next Sunday when Father Baehr will speak on the respect we should display for life. Let us stand now and pray."

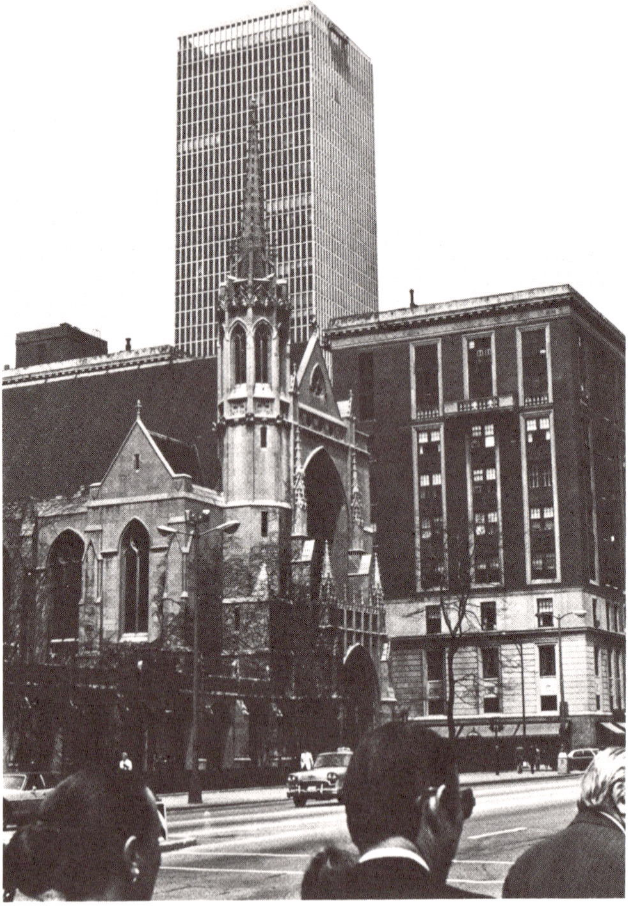

PART IV:
Concluding Rites

Concluding Rite

The concluding rite consists of:

a) the priest's greeting and blessing which is on certain days and occasions expanded by the prayer over the people or other solemn form;

b) the dismissal which sends each member of the congregation to do good works, praising and blessing the Lord.

—*The Roman Missal,* General Instruction

28. Go in Peace to Love and Serve the Lord

As a youngster I remember jumping up from the table after I had finished my meal, eager to run off and play with friends. A stern parental voice quickly ordered me back down in the chair and suggested that I first ask to be excused. When this ritual had been discharged, I was then permitted to leave, sent away on my mission of pleasure.

Leaving Mass early without cause bears a resemblance to the rude and self-centered action of an immature child.

The liturgy's concluding rite, extremely brief and to the point, serves as our formal "leave-taking," so to speak, in which we thank our host, the Lord, receive God's blessing and are sent forth with a particular task or mission to accomplish.

* "The Lord be with you," the priest's greeting at the start of this section, has a multiple meaning. It indicates this is a distinct portion of the celebration quite separate from, although connected with, the preceding elements. The greeting, in addition, reminds us, as it did when Mass began, that we have God within us through grace. However, it recalls we now have the additional presence of Christ's Word and Body in our hearts because of the liturgy.

* The priest's blessing dates back to the 12th or 13th century. It reads, "May almighty God bless you," not us, which seems to have developed recently among some celebrants. This invocation by the leader of worship who formally asks the Lord's benediction upon the congregation before him may now be expanded by one of 20 solemn blessings or 26 prayers over the people. Our experience shows that the priest's proper inflection and suitable pause give the community sufficient awareness of when to respond, "Amen."

* The three dismissals include the double notion of end and beginning. "The Mass is ended," but now we "go in peace," sent forth "in the peace of Christ," and seek "to love and serve the Lord." Those texts are either exact restorations from ancient Mass formulas or a combination of scriptural and early liturgical phrases.

Our term Mass, of course, comes from the Latin, "Ite, missa est": "Go, it is over" or completed or finished. That literal translation, nevertheless does not quite convey the full meaning. The elements of dismissal and even mission are also present. These concepts have been made explicit in the present Roman Missal's three formulas.

* The celebrant kisses the altar as a farewell gesture, just as he greeted that same holy stone representing Christ when he first entered the sanctuary.

* The liturgy should flow over into our lives afterwards. "To love and serve the Lord" certainly means to love and serve Christ in our neighbor.

The celebrant can make a fine start in that direction by standing at the main entrance of the church after Mass and greeting his people as they file out.

A coffee, cookie and conversation hour in an adjoining church or school hall also helps to link Sunday worship with the congregation's personal worlds.

Finally, in what I predict will become standard practice throughout the United States within a decade, desig-

Concluding Rites

nated lay persons could after Mass carry the Eucharist to those confined at home. Sharing the scriptural readings, homily and parish bulletin with these sick persons, praying by their side, distributing the sacred host to them, and visiting with such often unvisited people surely is a perfect way "to love and serve the Lord."